THIS JOURNAL BELONGS TO

....

Jesus, Name Above All Names

A Devotional Journal

ISBN 978-1-935416-26-5

Printed in China

JESUS
NAME ABOVE
ALL NAMES

A Devotional Journal

...inspired by life

THE TRUE LIGHT

*The one who is the true light, who gives light
to everyone, was coming into the world.*
JOHN 1:9 NLT

One night, in one place, one special star appeared in the heavens.
All the other stars in the night sky were lights declaring the glory of
God, but the light of His star appeared to point the way to the one
True Light. The other stars spoke of the great work of Creation,
but His star proclaimed the coming of the Creator to earth.

God still guides seeking hearts to the one True Light. As the world
around us grows darker, the Light of Jesus Christ shines even brighter.
He is a Light of truth, of hope, of purity, and of beauty. That Light
shines through the faces of those who know Him, through the eyes of
those who see Him, through the character of those who walk
with Him, and through the hearts of those who love Him.

A SON GIVEN

Unto us a Son is given.

ISAIAH 9:6 NKJV

When Jesus entered the world as a baby He was God come in the flesh. He was Mary's baby, but He was God's Son. The Creator entered creation as a man. Why did He do it? He came because His Father sent Him— not to impress us with His miracle power so that He could entertain us, not to educate us so that we could learn more facts about heaven, and not to provide us with new rituals so that we could become more religious. He came because we had sinned and needed to be forgiven, because the only way that we could ever be reconciled to God was by His Son coming and offering up His body as a sacrifice for our redemption.

What incredible love is in the heart of God for you and me. Jesus came as a visible expression of that love. Nothing is deeper than that love.

LAMB OF GOD

Behold the Lamb of God!
JOHN 1:36

On a quiet hillside close to where Jesus was born, God made the
news known. He spoke it in phrases of wonder, through creatures
of splendor, to men of low degree. Those who were excluded from
society's fancy gatherings would be included in heaven's greatest
celebration. Those who had little education would come to
know heaven's greatest revelation. Those who had few possessions
would come to receive heaven's greatest gift.

What greater witnesses could there be to the coming of the
Lamb of God than those who tended their flocks by night. Like
the shepherds, God comes to us in our spiritual nighttime to call
us to His light. He comes in our spiritual poverty to call us to the
riches in His Son. He comes in our spiritual loneliness to call us
to the fellowship of His eternal celebration.

THE WORD

The Word was made flesh, and dwelt among us.
JOHN 1:14

It has been said that the New Testament is concealed in the
Old Testament; the Old Testament is revealed in the New Testament.
In the Old we hear the voice of the prophets, in the New
we hear the voice of the Son. Together, the books tell one story.
It is His story. It is the story of redemption revealed in time
and space, through real people and actual events. It is the story
of the Redeemer and the redeemed.

In Jesus Christ the Old and New Testaments are like two musical
movements that come together to make one glorious symphony;
they are like the two lenses on a pair of binoculars that bring the image
close and into focus; they are like the flames of two burning candles
that come together to make one glorious light.

PROVIDER

My God shall supply all your need according
to his riches in glory by Christ Jesus.
PHILIPPIANS 4:19

From the beginning, it has been in the heart of God to meet the needs
of people. One of God's names is "The Lord Provides." He provides
because He cares, because He loves, and because He is faithful.
Redemption was God's plan to meet our greatest needs—the need
to be saved, to be forgiven, to fulfill God's purpose and plan for
our lives, and to be brought back into fellowship with Him.

When Jesus met people's needs He was teaching us important lessons
about His kingdom and showing us important things about His ways.
He was helping us to understand that there are no limits with
God and no limitation to His power. He wants us to be contented,
totally resting within the arms of His loving care.

INTERCESSOR AND HIGH PRIEST

Wherefore he is able also to save them to the uttermost
that come unto God by him, seeing he ever liveth
to make intercession for them.
HEBREWS 7:25

Jesus lived prayer and taught prayer. He prayed at different times and for various amounts of time. He prayed in secret and He prayed in public. He prayed about personal matters and matters concerning others. He prayed for His friends and for His enemies. He prayed as a man dependent upon His Father, seeking to please Him and glorify Him in all things.

Through prayer He drew near to His Father so that He could draw us nearer to His heart. He knelt in humility so that He could raise us up to new heights. He poured out His soul so that He could comfort us in every sorrow. As our High Priest, He prayed for our unity, our sanctification, our joy, our love, our keeping, our ministry, and our future purpose.

SON OF MAN

The Son of Man did not come to be served, but to serve,
and to give His life a ransom for many.

MATTHEW 20:28 NASB

Jesus came to serve and to give His life so that we could be loosed
from the power of sin and delivered from the power of Satan. He came
because He loved us, and He knew how much we needed Him.
He came to the lowly place so that He could lift us to the
highest place. He became poor in earthly things so that He
could make us rich in heavenly things.

Jesus laid aside His glory and took up our humanity. He laid aside
the praises of the heavenly host and made Himself of no reputation.
He laid aside His heavenly home and dined in the home of sinners.
He laid down His rights as God and took up a towel and a basin. He laid
aside the splendor of His throne and endured the shame of the cross.

SERVANT

For you know the grace of our Lord Jesus Christ, that
though He was rich, yet for your sakes He became poor,
that you through His poverty might become rich.

2 CORINTHIANS 8:9 NKJV

Imagine a large room filled with people. Each person has great needs
and is looking to the other people in the room to help fill those needs.
Each person thinks, "Here I am. I have arrived. I have many needs.
I am expecting each of you to do your very best to make me happy."
That is how all of us have lived our lives. We have not lived to serve,
but to be served.

When Jesus came to us, He was like a man who entered a room full of
needy people. However, Jesus said, "There you are. How may I serve
you? You do not have to give Me a reason to love you, for I love you
unconditionally. I give you My all, willingly, happily, freely."

REDEEMER

Therefore doth my Father love me, because I lay down my life, that I might take it again. No man taketh it from me, but I lay it down of myself. I have power to lay it down, and I have power to take it again. This commandment have I received of my Father.

JOHN 10:17-18

Who sent Jesus to the cross? Was it the Jewish leaders? Was it a mob? Was it the Roman government? None of these were powerful enough, influential enough, or persuasive enough to be able to do it. When Jesus spoke to Pilate, Jesus reminded him that he had no power to crucify Him even though Pilate thought he did as the Roman ruler.

The One who sent Jesus to the cross was God the Father. The cross was the reason God sent His Son into the world. It was the will of Jesus to embrace the Father's will. Jesus said that it was for this reason that He came.

INDESCRIBABLE GIFT

Thanks be to God for His indescribable gift!

2 CORINTHIANS 9:15 NASB

God's indescribable gift is not peace or joy, although His indescribable gift brings peace and joy. His gift is a person. His gift is Jesus Christ. When we have Jesus we have everything. All that our hearts have ever desired, every need we face, every truth we seek, and every blessing we long for is found in Jesus Christ. There is no other person, no other relationship, no other provision, and no other source that God will use to meet our deepest needs.

What a love! What a Savior! What a gift! May our hearts be open to receive Him, may our faith be ready to trust Him, may our wills be surrendered to obey Him, may our feet and hands be committed to follow Him, may our actions and attitudes be righteous to honor Him, and may our voices be uplifted to praise Him...now and forever.

JESUS

*Behold, thou shalt conceive in thy womb, and bring forth
a son, and shalt call his name JESUS.*

LUKE 1:31

When the angel Gabriel came to Mary to tell her the incredible news
of the life that would be formed in her, the angel also gave her the
name of the child. The name was not her choice, nor the choice of
Joseph, to whom she was espoused. The name was God's choice.
God chose a name that could, in one single word, put a spotlight on
the reason why God's Son left heaven and came to earth.

The earthly name God chose for His Son was "Jesus." In Hebrew
His name is Yeshua. Yeshua is not only a name that means salvation,
but it also means a celebration of all that salvation brings to us.
Even though Jesus could help people, heal people, guide people,
encourage people, and bless people, it would mean nothing if
He could not save people from their sins.

SAVIOR

*And we have seen and testify that the Father
has sent the Son as Savior of the world.*

1 JOHN 4:14 NKJV

Salvation means liberty from sin's bondage, forgiveness from sin's transgression, justification from sin's judgment, and life from sin's sentence of death. The celebration of salvation also means deliverance, aid, prosperity, health, help, and welfare. In sin we find everything that is bad, but in salvation we find everything that is good. In sin we find everything that is false; in salvation we find everything that is true.

Jesus was given the name Savior, because He is the Savior. Salvation is not found in a ritual, a church, a creed, or in any good works that anyone can do, no matter how sincere they may be. Salvation is in a person. God has only one Savior for the sinner, and one way to be saved. That way, that name, that person, is Jesus.

THE CHRIST

And Jacob begat Joseph the husband of Mary,
of whom was born Jesus, who is called Christ.

MATTHEW 1:16

The name Christ means Messiah. Messiah means the Anointed One, the One sent by God to be the Savior. For centuries the Jewish people had known through the promises God made to Abraham, Moses, and David that Messiah would come. Isaiah proclaimed, "His name shall be called Wonderful, Counsellor, The mighty God, The everlasting Father, The Prince of Peace."

The name Jesus Christ means that He is the Savior of all who believe, the promised Messiah, and the anointed redeemer of Israel. He is the one God so faithfully promised. Jesus was sent by the God of Israel; He did not send Himself. Jesus knew why He was sent; no one had to tell Him. His place, His person, His position, His passion, His purpose, flowed out of the anointing He carried as Messiah, the one sent by God.

THE LORD

And they said, Believe on the Lord Jesus Christ,
and thou shalt be saved, and thy house.
ACTS 16:31

The name "Lord" is an awesome name. It is a name that causes us to lift up our eyes and bend our knees, to raise our hands and humble our hearts, to celebrate with our voices and to worship in our spirits with reverential awe. Jesus Christ is not just the Lord, but He is the Lord of lords. He is the Master of all there is and the Ruler of all that will be.

When Jesus comes into a life as the Lord, He doesn't come in
to make suggestions, to plead His cause, to pamper or beg,
to argue or debate, to manipulate or bargain, to push or persuade,
to pamper or coddle. He comes into a life to take over.

Lord, teach me Your ways, guide my steps, and conform me
to Your image.

IMMANUEL, GOD WITH US

*"The virgin will be with child and will give birth
to a son, and they will call him Immanuel"
—which means, "God with us."*

MATTHEW 1:23 NIV

Immanuel means that God (deity) came to be with us (humanity).
God did not come to us as an idea, a concept, a philosophy, or an ideal.
He didn't come as the sun, the moon, or a star. He came to us as
a man. He took on human flesh. Jesus Christ is completely God
and completely man.

God with us—not in heaven, not out of touch or out of reach,
not a legend or a myth. God with us in grace, in truth, in mercy.
God with us in human flesh, touchable, seeable, knowable; walking
where we walk, crying our tears, feeling our grief, bearing our sorrows.
God with us—to believe in, to follow, to proclaim, to seek, to worship,
to love, to cherish forever!

WONDERFUL

For unto us a child is born, unto us a son is given:
and the government shall be upon his shoulder:
and his name shall be called Wonderful.

ISAIAH 9:6

Jesus is wonderful and does wonderful things. He is marvelous and does marvelous things. What He does flows out of who He is. He cannot deny Himself. Every name He bears is an extension of His person.

Because Jesus is wonderful, wonderful things happen to those who put their trust in Him. He will keep everyone who trusts in Him at the edge of their seat, with mouths open wide in utter astonishment, as He daily performs His wondrous works—wonders of mercy, wonders of grace, wonders of power, wonders of goodness, wonders of love. His wonders cannot be duplicated because they go beyond man's capabilities, accomplishing what man is unable to accomplish, achieving what man is unable to achieve.

Jesus Christ is wondrously, wonderfully, wonderful!

COUNSELOR

For unto us a Child is born, unto us a Son is given:
and the government shall be upon His shoulder:
and His name shall be called...Counselor.
ISAIAH 9:6 NKJV

Isn't it good to know that Jesus is your Counselor? He is never too busy
to see you. He is never late for an appointment. He is never in a rush
to get you out of the office. And He doesn't charge by the hour!

What a joyous privilege you have to be able to freely go to the One
who has all wisdom, knowledge, and understanding for the answers
you need in life. He knows your heart better than you do and knows
exactly what you need. You can go to Jesus as your Counselor because
He will always guide you in the right direction. He will counsel you
to think as He thinks, to feel as He feels, to walk as He walks,
to love as He loves, and to live as He lives.

MIGHTY GOD

Who is this King of glory?
The Lord strong and mighty,
the Lord mighty in battle.

PSALM 24:8

Jesus bears a name that only God can claim.
Men and angels can have might,
but only One is Mighty God.
No man, angel, or any created being
can be called Mighty God.
Mighty God means that Jesus doesn't sit
in the number-one place of power,
but He sits in the only place of ultimate power.
Jesus is the Strong One.
Jesus is the Conqueror that cannot be conquered.
He is Champion without a rival.

EVERLASTING FATHER

*Before the mountains were brought forth, or ever
thou hadst formed the earth and the world, even from
everlasting to everlasting, thou art God.*

PSALM 90:2

Everything in Jesus and about Jesus is everlasting. He is not a
temporary Savior who is filling in until someone else comes along.
Nothing about Him will go out of date or become irrelevant.
In the world, things wear off, wear out, die out, or dry up. The fun
or pleasure that people experience at a party soon leaves them,
and so they seek out a new party or experience that will bring them
some measure of momentary satisfaction. But, the reality of
Jesus Christ in our hearts never becomes stale, dry, empty, or
meaningless. Jesus is everlasting joy, not momentary happiness.

All that Jesus was to you yesterday He is today. All that He is to you
today He will always be, and more so as time goes by.

THE PRINCE OF PEACE

The Lord will give strength unto his people;
the Lord will bless his people with peace.

PSALM 29:11

Peace is not the absence of conflict, but the presence of Jesus.
Peace is not circumstantial, but relational. Peace is not based on
what is going on around you, but on Who is living in you.

Jesus did not come into your heart to bring you worry, anxiety, or
restlessness. He came to give you rest. His peace will guard your
thoughts from worry and keep your heart from fear.

"Be careful for nothing; but in every thing by prayer and supplication
with thanksgiving let your requests be made known unto God.
And the peace of God, which passeth all understanding, shall keep
your hearts and minds through Christ Jesus" (Philippians 4:6-7).

THE MAN OF SORROWS

He is despised and rejected of men; a man of sorrows,
and acquainted with grief: and we hid as it were our faces
from him; he was despised, and we esteemed him not.

ISAIAH 53:3

Jesus sought the lowly place so that He could lift you up. He was
rejected so that you could be accepted. He was acquainted with
grief so that you could be comforted.

One of the ways that we see the heart of Jesus is through His
meekness. Meekness is not weakness. His meekness means that
He was totally submitted to the will of the Father. He who is
Almighty and could have called an army of angels to rescue Him,
chose instead to learn obedience through the things He suffered.

Meekness is heard in this prayer that Jesus prayed, "Not my will,
but thine be done." The meekness, the sorrow, and the suffering of
Jesus mean that you never need to question His love for you.

THE ADVOCATE

My little children, these things write I unto you,
that ye sin not. And if any man sin, we have an advocate
with the Father, Jesus Christ the righteous.

1 JOHN 2:1

Jesus, as your advocate, is the one who pleads your case. He is your comforter in heaven, just as the Holy Spirit is your comforter on earth. He who knows your sins is also the one who has identified Himself with your sins. His voice pleads on your behalf as your Righteous Redeemer.

Satan's accusations against you are many. As your Advocate, Jesus does not plead your innocence, but He presents the irrefutable evidence of the atonement that He has made on your behalf. As someone once said, "When you ask Jesus to represent you as your heavenly lawyer, remember that He has never lost a case."

THE ALPHA AND OMEGA

I am Alpha and Omega, the beginning and the ending, saith the Lord, which is, and which was, and which is to come, the Almighty.

Jesus is the first and last—
He has the first and last word in our decisions;
His direction is the beginning point of our journey;
His destination is the place we need to arrive;
His has the final say in every conversation.
He holds first place in our hearts.
He is our first priority and final authority;
He is our first and only option;
He starts and ends things in our lives.
He sustains us and brings things to completion.
He is the sunrise of our morning;
He is the sunset of our day;
His mercy greets us in the morning;
His goodness covers us in the night.

THE BREAD OF LIFE

Then Jesus said unto them, Verily, verily, I say unto you,
Moses gave you not that bread from heaven;
but my Father giveth you the true bread from heaven.
JOHN 6:32

Bread is made to be eaten, not to be set on a shelf and admired.
Jesus is the spiritual Bread we eat. All who are spiritually hungry
have been called to partake of the life of Jesus by faith.

Jesus is God's manna to us. Like the manna came down from heaven,
so Jesus came to us from the Father. Jesus is the perfect food,
full of every spiritual nutrient. He is fresh food, meeting our
needs every morning and sustaining us through the day.

"I am that bread of life" (John 6:48).

THE BELOVED

For he received from God the Father honour and glory,
when there came such a voice to him from the excellent glory,
This is my beloved Son, in whom I am well pleased.
2 PETER 1:17

Jesus is the Father's "Beloved." He spoke that name over Him when
John baptized Jesus. God also spoke that name over Him when Jesus was
on the Mount of Transfiguration. Each time the name "Beloved" was
spoken, it was followed by the words, "In whom I am well pleased."

Jesus wants us to trust Him to live His life in us. The life that Jesus
lives in us is the life that will always be pleasing to the Father.

"To the praise of the glory of his grace, wherein he hath made
us accepted in the beloved" (Ephesians 1:6).

THE ARM OF THE LORD

The Lord hath made bare his holy arm in the eyes
of all the nations; and all the ends of the earth
shall see the salvation of our God.

ISAIAH 52:10

"The Arm of the Lord" is such an awesome name. Through this name
God is telling us that His Son is the extension of His might and the
expression of His heart. His arm has the power to anoint the eyes of
a blind man and restore his sight. His arm has the tenderness to
embrace a little child and draw him to His side.

The arm of the Lord also reminds us of the tender care of the Lord.
It is His strong arm that can lift us, hold us, and keep us close to
His heart. The arm of the Lord is extended, not to forbid you access
to His grace, but to pour His grace upon you in abundance.

As the caring Shepherd carries the lost lamb in his arms,
so the Lord carries us.

THE FOUNDATION

Therefore thus saith the Lord Gᴏᴅ, Behold, I lay in Zion for
a foundation a stone, a tried stone, a precious corner stone,
a sure foundation: he that believeth shall not make haste.

ISAIAH 28:16

Lives that are built upon poor foundations will collapse in the storms
of life. Jesus is the only one we can build our lives upon and not face
ruin. He is the solid foundation of our faith. The Bible tells us that
God will shake everything that is shakable; only what cannot be
shaken will remain. Nothing you have in Christ can be lost or
destroyed when you stand upon His solid ground.

Let your life stand on Christ, for His foundation is unshakable.
Let your hope rest in Christ, for His foundation is unmovable.
Let your heart trust in Christ, for His foundation is indestructible.

OUR PASSOVER

Christie, our Passover, was sacrificed for us.

1 CORINTHIANS 5:7 NKJV

Christ our Passover is a powerful truth. It tells us that what God did for Israel when the blood of the slain lamb was applied to the doorposts of their homes, God will do for us when we apply, by faith, the blood of the slain Lamb of God to the doorposts of our hearts. The result of the applied blood of the lamb was that Israel was saved from the wrath of God that fell upon Egypt in the judgment of death. Jesus our Passover means that in Him we will be saved from the coming wrath of God and His final judgment upon the disobedient.

Our deliverance from God's wrath is a real thing. If God's deliverance is real, God's judgment is also real. We can thank God every day that He has extended His mercy to us; that the blood of His Son, our Passover, has been sacrificed for us.

THE TREASURE

For it is the God who commanded light to shine out of darkness, who has shone in our hearts to give the light of the knowledge of the glory of God in the face of Jesus Christ. But we have this treasure in earthen vessels.

2 CORINTHIANS 4:6-7 NKJV

People often ask the question, "What's life all about?" Thankfully, God had the answer to that question long before anyone asked it. To put it simply, it's all about Jesus.

What's life all about? It's about the treasure, not the vessel. It's about His glory, not our looks; it's about His love, not our niceness. It's about His purpose, not our plans; it's about His kingdom, not our agenda. It's about His reign, not our rights; it's about His truth, not our opinions; it's about His will, not our way. It's about His life, not our efforts.

THE SEED

What, then, was the purpose of the law? It was added
because of transgressions until the Seed to whom
the promise referred had come.

GALATIANS 3:19 NIV

The other day, I walked out my front door and there, near the
southwest corner of my house, stood a strange looking plant.
Upon further examination I concluded that it must be a corn stalk.
I couldn't imagine how it got there, but there it was. My son
told me he'd been feeding some corn to a few wild deer that
had been visiting our property.

To my surprise a few ears of corn were starting to form.
My house is not in Iowa, and my yard is no cornfield, but that
kernel of corn didn't care. When Jesus, the Seed, gets planted
in your heart, it will do what seed is supposed to do. It will
start off small, but it won't take long before others start
noticing that something new is growing in your life.

ALMIGHTY ONE

I am...the Almighty One.
REVELATION 1:8 NLT

Isn't it wonderful to know that you belong to someone who is Almighty?
It means that Jesus Christ is without limitations. He rules, He reigns,
He is in control, He can handle anything, and He can do anything.
Once you know this, you must never put any limits on what
He wants to do in your life.

No one can intimidate the Almighty, push Him around, or bully Him.
No one has that kind of power, authority, or influence. The Almighty
fears no man, is not threatened by any one's objective, and is never
forced to cancel any of His plans.

Jesus is mighty enough to keep anything or anyone from getting in
the way of His will for you. No one has the power to stop His plan
for your life. When Jesus says to you, "Follow Me," no one can
overrule Him. Jesus has the final say. Period!

LIGHT OF THE WORLD

*Then Jesus spoke to them again, saying, "I am the
light of the world. He who follows Me shall not walk
in darkness, but have the light of life."*

JOHN 8:12 NKJV

The world is a dark place, but there is a Light that shines brighter than
any lighthouse and can save any battered vessel from being smashed
against the rocks of sin. The light of Jesus will always take you out of
the darkness of selfishness, evil, fear, confusion, bondage, and dead
religion. There are many false lights who say, "Look to me. Listen to me.
Follow me." But as we heed the voice of "false lights" (2 Corinthians
11:14) we only go deeper into the darkness.

Jesus said that His light is the light of life. He lights up the deepest
place within us—where we live, move, and have our being. When
His light is in us we are spiritually alive.

AMEN

These are the words of the Amen.

REVELATION 3:14 NIV

When we hear the word "amen" we often think of it as the end to a prayer. We wait to hear it as a clue that the person who is praying has finished. When Jesus says He is the "Amen" it means something far greater. It means that everything He is and has to say we can be certain about. When Jesus says "Amen" to His words, He is saying that He is the fulfillment of everything He has said.

In modern language we use a phrase like "you can count on it" as a way of convincing someone that what we have said is reliable, dependable, and trustworthy. "Amen" is that and more. "Amen" is the vow, the guarantee, and the oath of God stating that everything that has been said has been sealed with a binding promise. Have you read something today in Scripture that Jesus has said to you? You can count on it. Amen!

ANOINTED ONE

You know of Jesus of Nazareth, how God anointed
Him with the Holy Spirit and with power.

ACTS 10:38 NASB

There is only one Anointed One, only one Messiah, only one Christ,
only one Savior that God recognizes. All of these names are found
in one person, the Lord Jesus Christ.

For many years, if a manufacturer wanted to make sure his product
would be accepted by the public as legitimate, reliable, and dependable,
he would hope to receive the Good Housekeeping Seal of approval.
God's Anointed One means that Jesus Christ has received God's Divine
Seal of approval. God will never give that approval to anyone else.

The anointed ministry of Jesus Christ is available to you today. Through
the power of the Holy Spirit, He still releases the captive, and brings
the free gift of God's salvation to all who call upon His name.

APOSTLE

Wherefore, holy brethren, partakers of the heavenly calling, consider the Apostle...Christ Jesus.
HEBREWS 3:1

One of the meanings of an apostle is someone who is sent from one place to another as an ambassador. An ambassador is an official representative of the highest rank. Jesus Christ is our "sent one."

When people are in danger or trouble, a rescue team will be sent out to bring them back to safety. As a young boy living on the east coast, I went with my mother for a vacation at the beach. During our visit we were caught in a powerful hurricane. When my uncle learned of the danger we were in he immediately came to rescue us.

God the Father sent His Son to rescue you. Jesus told His disciples that He was sending them into the world in the same way the Father had sent Him (John 20:21). Jesus has called you to be His "sent one" and represent Him to the world as His ambassador.

AUTHOR AND FINISHER OF OUR FAITH

Looking unto Jesus the author and finisher of our faith.
HEBREWS 12:2

We have often heard the comment, "You can start well, but you must also finish well." This can leave us with a wrong impression that Jesus starts our Christian life for us, but it's up to us to finish it.

We start out our Christian life by focusing our faith on the finished work of Christ upon the cross. We maintain the Christian life by focusing our faith upon the risen Christ. We carry a hope for our future by focusing our faith upon the second coming of Christ. Past, present, and future are all tied up in Christ alone.

We start well, live well, and finish well by keeping the eyes of our faith fixed upon Jesus. Jesus is the starting point and the ending point of our faith journey. You will finish well, not by seeing how many good things you can do, but by never taking your eyes off Jesus.

BISHOP

For ye were as sheep going astray; but are now returned unto the Shepherd and Bishop of your souls.

1 PETER 2:25

Jesus is watching over your soul, not just your physical needs. He cares about your well-being, your wholeness, and your wellness. He is looking out for your physical, emotional, and spiritual needs.

It is important for us to remember that the title of Shepherd and Bishop has already been given to and claimed by Jesus Christ. No one can be given this title in the church apart from Him. The Chief Shepherd and Bishop of your soul is Jesus Christ. Those who use these titles are responsible to represent Him well. They must oversee the flock as Jesus oversees the flock; they must care for the sheep as Jesus cares for the sheep. There is only one Good Shepherd who lays down His life for the sheep, and every under-shepherd needs to know His heartbeat.

THE BRIDEGROOM

He who has the bride is the bridegroom; but the groomsman who stands by and listens to him rejoices greatly and heartily on account of the bridegroom's voice.

JOHN 3:29 AMP

I was recently at the wedding of a member of our family. The parents, grandparents, and special family members were ushered in and took their seats. Next, the groomsmen came out and walked the bridesmaids down the aisle to their designated place. With excitement and expectation, everyone waited for the entrance of the bride.

As the music played, the bride entered the back of the church. And as the heads of everyone turned toward the bride, my attention shifted to the bridegroom. As she moved toward him, his eyes were fixed upon her. His face beamed with delight. The closer she came the more he glowed. He couldn't wait to make her his own. That moment helped me realize how much Jesus is looking forward to the Marriage Supper of the Lamb and the coming of His bride, the church.

BRIGHT AND MORNING STAR

I, Jesus, have sent My angel to testify to you these things in the churches. I am the Root and the Offspring of David, the Bright and Morning Star.

REVELATION 22:16 NKJV

When in an airplane on a dark and cloudy day, it's always exciting to break through the clouds into the bright sunlight that shines above them. Jesus is the sunlight in your day, and He is much more. As the Bright and Morning Star, He bathes the start of your day in brightness.

Sometimes, when I get up in the morning, I sense that a spirit of darkness or heaviness has come upon me during the night. This sense of darkness, whatever the source, does not have to set the tone for my day. Jesus is my reality, and each morning He is my Bright and Morning Star. The brightness of Jesus' name means that He makes the beginning of each day magnificently clear and good.

COMMANDER OF THE LORD'S ARMY

And it came to pass, when Joshua was by Jericho, that he lifted his eyes and looked, and behold, a Man stood opposite him with His sword drawn in His hand.... Then the Commander of the LORD's army said to Joshua, "Take your sandal off your foot, for the place where you stand is holy."

JOSHUA 5:13-15

When Joshua met the Lord, Joshua assumed He was a common warrior, not the Divine Warrior. Joshua was in for a huge surprise. He was not confronting a human figure, but the pre-incarnate Son of God. Joshua attempted to find out which side this warrior was on, but he discovered that the Commander of the Lord's Army did not come to take sides, but to take over. Joshua did not meet a high-ranking military officer, but the Commander and Chief of heaven's army. It didn't take Joshua long to discover that he was not on a battleground, but on holy ground.

MIGHTY WARRIOR

*Now thanks be unto God, which always causeth
us to triumph in Christ, and maketh manifest the
savour of his knowledge by us in every place.*
2 CORINTHIANS 2:14

Jesus is your Mighty Warrior in every battle of life that you face.
He has come to take over and be in charge of every circumstance
you face. The next time you consider who is against you, quickly
turn your attention to who is for you—the Father, the Son,
the Holy Spirit, the heavenly host, the body of Christ, and the
prayers of God's people are all on your side. You cannot lose for
He is victorious. You cannot be defeated for He has conquered all.
You cannot fail for He will always lead you into triumph.

"We are more than conquerors through
him that loved us" (Romans 8:37).

CAPTAIN OF SALVATION

For it was fitting for Him, for whom are all things and by whom are all things, in bringing many sons to glory, to make the captain of their salvation perfect through sufferings.
HEBREWS 2:10 NKJV

It is dangerous to follow someone if they are taking you in the wrong direction. The Bible calls false leaders "the blind leading the blind." As captain of our salvation, Jesus leads the way to the eternal city and its glorious riches. Jesus is the Pioneer, blazing the trail to heaven's door. He knows the way through the wilderness of sin, through the darkness of this world, through the traps and snares of the deceiver, through the quicksand of lies and deception, through the folly of lustful pleasures, and through the idolatry of false gods and empty worship. As a follower of Jesus Christ you are a member of His holy band of brothers and sisters whom God is leading from glory to glory.

LIFE

Jesus said to him, "I am the way, the truth, and the life. No one comes to the Father except through Me."

JOHN 14:6 NKJV

Every day, for each of us, life happens—people oversleep, burn the toast, hurt their backs, get an emergency phone call, have a flat tire, lose their keys, miss a flight, catch a cold, or experience a thousand-and-one other unexpected things. When we say "life happens" what we are really saying is "circumstances happen."

Jesus said that He is the Life (the reality). Circumstances happen around us; the life of Jesus happens within us. The reality of Jesus Christ is greater than the reality of our circumstances. Jesus' reality should rule the heart of every believer. "Life" happens to everyone, but it is His reality that can keep us moving through life in quietness, in confidence, in righteousness, in peace, in strength, and in joy. When "life happens" let "Jesus happen" in you.

CARPENTER

Is not this the Carpenter, the son of Mary and the brother of James and Joses and Judas and Simon?

MARK 6:3 AMP

There's a bumper sticker that reads, "My Boss Is a Jewish Carpenter." The name "Carpenter" tells us a lot about Jesus as a man—including His training, His skills, and His ability to work with wood. In a spiritual sense, we can also look at Jesus as a Carpenter. He is the one who is building your life with the skill of a Master Craftsman. He knows where to cut, where to sand the rough spots, where to chisel, how to straighten crooked boards, how to apply the right amount of pressure to shape the wood, where to join things together, and how to apply a lasting finish. As He does His work within you, He does so with the finished work in view. And He knows exactly what He needs to do in order to bring that work to completion.

CHIEF SHEPHERD

When the Chief Shepherd appears, you will receive
the crown of glory that does not fade away.
1 PETER 5:4 NKJV

One of the challenges we have in life is being able to talk with the
right person when we need to get something done. Often, when we
call a large company with an important issue that needs attention,
we discover that the person we are talking to can't really help us. If we
press the matter, we can be passed off to different people along the line,
but in the process we rarely get connected with the person who is
actually empowered to take action and make a final decision.

As the sheep of His pasture, the Lord has told us who is in charge.
Jesus Christ is not only the Good Shepherd of the sheep, but He is also
the True Shepherd, the Great Shepherd, and the Chief Shepherd.
As your Chief Shepherd, He makes sure that you have all you need.

CHIEF (PRECIOUS) CORNERSTONE

For thus it stands in Scripture: Behold, I am laying in Zion a chosen (honored), precious chief Cornerstone, and he who believes in Him [who adheres to, trusts in, and relies on Him] shall never be disappointed or put to shame.

1 PETER 2:6 AMP

The cornerstone lines up a building in the same way that a point person lines up a group of marching soldiers. The cornerstone is the key foundation stone; it must be put in place first, before any other stone is added. All other stones will be set in reference to the cornerstone.

Jesus Christ is the Cornerstone of our faith, our life, and our future. The only safe way to build our lives is to line up each decision we make with our eyes fixed upon Jesus. We need to make sure that each step we take lines up with His perfect will for our lives; that is the only way to live life without regrets.

CHIEFEST AMONG TEN THOUSAND

My beloved is...the chiefest among ten thousand.
SONG OF SONGS 5:10

In our culture people are daily presented with multiple choices.
Ice cream shops offer dozens of flavors; clothes come in a wide variety
of colors and styles; satellite and cable companies have a variety of
TV packages; menus offer a wide range of entrées. There are a multitude
of gods, religions, sects, and cults to choose from—but Jesus Christ is
the only true God.

Jesus Christ is the best person anyone could know, but the knowledge
of Him does not come automatically. Jesus does not force Himself
upon anyone. Each of us has a choice to make and each person must
make a personal decision to know Him. We do not make a decision to
only know facts about Him, but to know Him personally and intimately.
He is truly the Chiefest Among Ten Thousand and is the best decision
anyone could ever make.

COVENANT OF THE PEOPLE

*I the LORD have called thee in righteousness,
and will...give thee for a covenant of the people.*

ISAIAH 42:6

The Scripture above is a powerful reminder to us of who Jesus is and
what He has done. God's covenant promise was spoken to us in His
word, but it was fulfilled in a person. Jesus is our covenant! God's
covenant promise to us will never be invalid because Jesus will never be
invalid. Because Jesus is the Truth, the covenant is the Truth; because
Jesus is eternal, the covenant is eternal; because Jesus is trustworthy,
the covenant is trustworthy.

God will never break His covenant promise because Jesus is the
"Yes" from God about His covenant with us and His promises to us.
Each morning you can arise and say, "The covenant is mine because
Jesus is mine; the covenant is certain because Jesus is certain;
the covenant is real because Jesus is real."

DAYSPRING

Through the tender mercy of our God,
With which the Dayspring from on high has visited us;
To give light to those who sit in darkness
and the shadow of death,
To guide our feet into the way of peace.

LUKE 1:78-79 NKJV

When the night is the darkest and the temperature
is the coldest, your hope can begin to soar.
It is at that moment that the first light
of a new day will soon appear before your eyes.
Are you going through a dark battle?
Does it seem as though the dawning of victory's light
will never come? Stand fast. Stand firm.
Stand confident and full of hope.
The Dayspring from on high is about to
shine over your situation. His light will show you
the next step to take, the way will become clear,
and the pathway of peace will open up before you.

DELIVERER

And so all Israel will be saved: as it is written,
"The Deliverer will come out of Zion."
ROMANS 11:26 NKJV

As a kid during the 1940s, I loved going to the Saturday afternoon matinees. Usually, there was a western movie, a bunch of cartoons, and a weekly serial. The hero in the serial always found himself in great danger at the very end of the episode. The following Saturday I would discover that my hero was miraculously delivered from the peril he was in the week before.

The Apostle Paul could have been the hero in the Saturday serials. Time and again, he found himself in great peril. Paul never would have been able to fulfill his calling and finish his course if he did not have a Deliverer to snatch him from danger. Paul tells us, "The Lord will deliver me from every evil attack and will bring me safely into his heavenly Kingdom" (2 Timothy 4:18 NLT).

THE DOOR

Then said Jesus unto them again, Verily, verily,
I say unto you, I am the door of the sheep.

JOHN 10:7

A popular TV quiz show would end its program by presenting the winning contestant with the option of opening one of three doors. Behind each door was a prize, but only one door held the grand prize.

There are three doors that none of us should seek to open. Behind each one is something very undesirable. The first is the door of the world; behind this door everything is passing away. The second is the door of the flesh; behind this door everything leads to death. The third is the door of the devil; behind this door everything brings darkness.

The Bible tells us that every spiritual blessing we could ever desire or need is found in Jesus Christ—every treasure, every gift, every joy. Jesus is the only Door that will lead you to life and all that is good.

FAITHFUL

Now I saw heaven opened, and behold, a white horse.
And He who sat on him was called Faithful...and in
righteousness He judges and makes war.
REVELATION 19:11 NKJV

All of us desire meaningful relationships where people can trust
one another. One of the hardest things to overcome in any relationship
is unfaithfulness. Once trust has been broken it is devastating.
There are other ways that trust can be broken. Some people say,
"I am having a hard time at work because I can't trust my boss."
Others say, "I trusted my friend with a deep secret, and I was
shocked to learn of their betrayal."

Jesus carries the name "Faithful" because He is worthy of our
complete trust and confidence. He will never let you down.
His words are true and that makes Him believable; His actions
are consistent and that makes Him dependable; His character is
without flaw and that makes Him indescribable!

TRUE

Now I saw heaven opened, and behold, a white horse.
And He who sat on him was called...True, and in
righteousness He judges and makes war.
REVELATION 19:11 NKJV

Jesus is true in His words, everything He says can be counted upon.
Jesus is true in His motives, everything He does is done for a right and
good reason. Jesus is true in His actions, everything He does is genuine.
There is no falsehood or deceit in Him. Jesus would never trick
someone, con them into believing something, playact, or speak about
fiction as though it were fact. Jesus is 100 percent genuine.

Jesus is true in His promises, true in His character, and true in
His attitudes. He is true in His faithfulness, true in His kindness,
and true in His love. He is also true in all His judgments.
No matter which way you observe Him, everything about
Him is true and bears witness to the truth.

FIRSTBORN FROM THE DEAD

Jesus Christ, the faithful witness, the firstborn from the dead,
and the ruler over the kings of the earth.

REVELATION 1:5 NKJV

Two men were hiking when the trail led them to the edge of a high cliff. In front of them stood a rickety old wooden bridge suspended across a raging river hundreds of feet below. Unless they crossed the bridge they could not continue their journey. Neither one wanted to test the bridge's safety by crossing first.

A group of Christians may all talk about the wonders of heaven, but most likely, no one wants to go first. Jesus knew the fear that each of us has about death. Because Jesus is the firstborn from the dead, He is assuring us that He not only tasted death, but He is also the first to rise from the dead. Through our death we will simply be following Him into our resurrection. Jesus has gone first and He is telling us that everything will be okay.

FORERUNNER

*Where Jesus has entered in for us...a Forerunner having become
a High Priest forever after the order...of Melchizedek.*
HEBREWS 6:20 AMP

When wagon trains crossed the country heading into the unknown
territory of the American west, they hired scouts (forerunners) to go
before them to find out what was ahead. Pioneers needed to know
where the trail would take them, if there were dangers ahead, and if
there was a good place to camp for the night. Most important of all,
the job of the scout was to make sure the travelers took the path that
would bring them safely to their final destination.

Jesus, as our forerunner, is the one who has gone before us and blazed
the trail to the Father's house. He has entered the sanctuary of heaven,
into the very presence of God, and has reported back to us with all
the information we need to arrive safely at our final destination.

OUR REST

But the Levitical priests...shall not gird themselves
with anything that causes [them to] sweat.
EZEKIEL 44:15, 18 AMP

In the Bible, a single word can be like a powerful spotlight that reveals
to our spiritual eyes a truth of gigantic proportions. The word "sweat"
that is used in Ezekiel 44 is one of those words.

The context of the word "sweat" ties back to the manner in which
the priests of the Lord were to minister to Him in the inner court.
The inner court was the place of God's presence, a place where
the Lord *rested*. It is through the shed blood of Jesus Christ
that the presence of the Lord has been opened to us. The work
of Redemption is Jesus' work alone; our own efforts (sweat)
can add nothing to His finished work.

God does not want us to serve Him out of the energy and efforts of
our flesh, but in the power and strength of the Holy Spirit.

OUR HOPE

Paul, an apostle of Jesus Christ by the commandment of God our Saviour, and Lord Jesus Christ, which is our hope.

1 TIMOTHY 1:1

Today we have a future hope. Our hope is not based upon anything man can do or say, but is based upon Jesus Christ—what He has said, what He has done, what He has yet to do. Our future is bright because His hope shines brightly in our hearts. This hope is not fixed upon where the world is going, but upon when Jesus is coming; not upon political leaders, but upon Jesus' reign and rule; not upon global solutions, but upon Jesus' eternal plan.

To keep our eyes on Jesus is to keep our eyes on hope. The eyes that look upon Him will never be downcast or in despair. Hope is not wishful thinking, but expectation in the promises that He has given us and in all the provisions that He has made for us.

OUR HELP

Why are you cast down, O my inner self? And why should
you moan over me and be disquieted within me?
Hope in God and wait expectantly for Him,
for I shall yet praise Him, my Help and my God.

PSALM 42:5 AMP

The world's political systems can only offer people a false hope.
The Bible tells us plainly that the world is going in the wrong
direction and moving there at a rapid pace. Jesus told those who
would follow Him not to expect things to be easy, "If the world
hates you, know that it hated Me before it hated you."

Today Jesus wants to be our help; He wants us to keep our hope
in Him and not in this world's system or its leaders. Jesus has us
here for an eternal purpose—to be a light of hope that needs to
be seen; to be a voice of truth that needs to be heard; to be a
demonstration of love that needs to be lived.

PRIEST

You are a priest forever in the order of Melchizedek.

HEBREWS 7:17 NLT

Jesus' priesthood was of a different order and brought about different results compared to the priesthood of Aaron.

The Levitical priests died and needed to be replaced; Jesus, our Priest, lives forever. The Levitical priests offered the blood of animals as an atonement for sin over and over again; Jesus, our Priest, offered His own blood as an atonement for our sin once and for all. The Levitical priests had to make an offering for their own sins; Jesus, our Priest, was without sin. The Levitical priesthood was identified with the old covenant; Jesus, our Priest, is identified with the new covenant. The Levitical priesthood was imperfect; Jesus' priesthood was perfect.

You can be absolutely assured that today, because Jesus is your Priest, He is able to save you. And He is, at this very moment, praying for you.

HEAD OF THE CHURCH

Christ is the Head of the church,
Himself the Savior of [His] body.
EPHESIANS 5:23 AMP

We were made, not for a life of independent living, but to be under the loving leadership of the One who made us. Isaiah reminds us that we have all gone astray and that each one of us has turned to his own way. Our own way is always the wrong way that takes us in the wrong direction. We cannot make it on our own; God never intended us to.

When the Bible tells us that Jesus is the Head of the church, it means that He is the head over a body of believers, not a church building. We are "living stones" that He fits together for His purposes. Individually and collectively, it is good for us to know Jesus has the right plan. Jesus, as the head of the church, is the one who is in complete charge. We are totally dependent upon Him.

HEIR OF ALL THINGS

In the last of these days He has spoken to us in [the person of a]
Son, Whom He appointed Heir and lawful Owner of all things.
HEBREWS 1:2 AMP

For many years, when my dad was alive, he would often start a letter
to me, "To Roy, heir of the Lessin millions." It would always make me
smile when I read it because I knew my dad didn't have any money.
It is one thing to be called an heir; it is quite another thing to actually
be the heir of something of great value.

God the Father has declared His Son to be the appointed Heir, and that
is no small thing. The inheritance is so great the Bible simply sums it
up by saying "the Heir of all things." What is even more amazing is to
realize that you, as God's child, are a joint-heir with Christ. That means
that you share directly in the inheritance that is His.

HOLY ONE

*For You will not leave my soul in Sheol, nor will
You allow Your Holy One to see corruption.*
PSALM 16:10 NKJV

During a cleaning project in our kitchen, I decided the cabinets needed
a fresh coat of paint. All of our kitchen cabinets were painted white.
At the paint store I was surprised to discover how many different shades
of white were available. Tints within the paint created a color range
that went from "off white" to "white white" with many in between.

When the Bible tells us that Jesus is the Holy One, it means that He is
"true whiteness" with all the tints (impurities) taken out. Every person
that we try to match up with the life, the character, and the nature of
Jesus Christ turns out looking soiled and dirty in comparison. The only
way we can be "holy" is not by trying to be better or live a cleaner,
"whiter" life, but by letting the Holy One live His life in us.

ETERNAL LIFE

The life appeared; we have seen it and testify to it,
and we proclaim to you the eternal life, which was
with the Father and has appeared to us.

1 JOHN 1:2 NIV

One of the greatest things the gospel of Jesus Christ gives to us is hope, especially when we are going through times of loss and mourning. The hope of the gospel is a blessed hope, uniquely tied to the resurrection of Christ from the dead.

When someone says, "I hope so," it is because there is uncertainty in what may happen. The hope that is ours in Jesus is a certainty, a reality, and a testimony. He is always right and we can trust His character.

Our hope is based upon historical fact, upon biblical promises, and upon a great cloud of witnesses who have given witness to the truth. Jesus is our hope of eternal life.

SANCTIFICATION

*But of him are ye in Christ Jesus, who of God
is made unto us wisdom, and righteousness,
and sanctification, and redemption.*

1 CORINTHIANS 1:30

God is the One who sanctifies His people through His Son, Jesus Christ.
If you were planning an elegant dinner, you would not only take out
the special plates that have been set aside for such an occasion, but you
would also wash them. Sanctification has two main applications to our
lives. One is that God sets us aside for His special use and purpose. The
second is that God also cleanses those whom He sets aside.

As God's sanctified child, you have been separated from the common
crowd to be one of His holy people. He wants your heart to be unmixed
in its motives and pure in its devotion. The beautiful thing
about sanctification is that you become conformed to the image
of the One you serve.

GOOD SHEPHERD

*I am the Good Shepherd; and I know and recognize
My own, and My own know and recognize Me.*
JOHN 10:14 AMP

Few names have been more endearing to the hearts of God's people
than the name "Shepherd." It is the name that invokes thoughts of
comfort, tenderness, care, and security. The name also creates strong
emotion within us because at its root the name means "to keep
company with, as with a friend."

The name "Shepherd" dries our tears and expels our fears. The Lord
is the shepherd of your soul, the keeper of your life, and the guardian
of your way. To shepherd is never part-time work. God will never take
His eye off you or leave you unattended. You are personally His and
He is personally yours. The Good Shepherd cares for you more than
anyone does and loves you more than anyone ever could.

I AM

*Jesus replied, I assure you, most solemnly I tell you,
before Abraham was born, I AM.*

JOHN 8:58 AMP

Jesus, the eternal "I Am," is the "I Am" of everything you need, of all
you desire, and of all you long to be. He is your wisdom, your authority,
and your confidence. He is your purpose, your hope, and your future.
When Jesus says "I Am" He is saying that He is all-in-all. He is your
provider and He is your provision, whatever your need may be.

He is your "I Am" when things are smooth and when things are rough;
when you are up and when you are down; when there is sunshine and
when there is rain. He is your "I Am" first thing in the morning, in the
middle of the day, in the evening shadows, and when you go to bed at
night. He is the "I Am" of every moment, of every ministry, of every
appointment, and of every circumstance.

UNSEARCHABLE RICHES

To me, who am less than the least of all the saints,
this grace was given, that I should preach
among the Gentiles the unsearchable riches of Christ.

EPHESIANS 3:8 NKJV

Do you know who you really are in Jesus Christ? Have you discovered
your true identity and are you living in the reality of it today?
You are the Lord's possession. He made you and He owns you.
He has ownership of you through creation and redemption.

You are His, wholly and completely. There are no doubts in His mind
or in heaven's records. The devil has no lien against your life. Because
of the purchase price that Jesus paid upon the cross, Satan has no
rightful claim upon you. Jesus became poor so you could become rich.
You have been lavished with riches—riches of grace, riches of mercy,
riches of kindness, riches of faith, riches of love, riches of salvation,
riches of glory, for now and forevermore.

THE IMAGE OF GOD

God...has in these last days spoken to us by His Son,
whom He has appointed heir of all things, through
whom also He made the worlds; who being the brightness
of His glory and the express image of His person.

HEBREWS 1:1-3 NKJV

Years ago there was a movie titled *The Invisible Man*. He lived
and moved about like everyone else, but no one could see him
or know his identity. Even though this man had thoughts,
feelings, desires, and a will, no image of the man appeared in
the mirror when he stood before it.

God is a person who thinks and feels. He has a personality, a nature,
and a character. He is love, He is holy, and He is true. One of the
many differences between God and the invisible man is that when
God looks in the mirror an image of His likeness does appear.
The image of God that appears is Jesus Christ.

DWELLING PLACE

Lord, You have been our dwelling place and our
refuge in all generations [says Moses].
PSALM 90:1 AMP

The Man Without a Country is a sad story that tells the plight of Philip
Nolan. He renounces the United States and is sentenced to spend
the rest of his life on warships, without the right to ever again
set foot on American soil.

One of the saddest stories in real life is the plight of the homeless who
live on city streets and in parks. These are people with a thousand
different stories to tell, but who all have one thing in common: the
absence of a place they can call "home."

The saddest story of all is to learn of someone who is spiritually
homeless. There is no greater emptiness, loneliness, or isolation
than this. Jesus Christ came to make His home within our hearts.
His presence makes it possible for every person to find their
true and eternal home with Him.

TABERNACLE

And the Word (Christ) became flesh (human, incarnate) and
tabernacled (fixed His tent of flesh, lived awhile) among us;
and we [actually] saw His glory (His honor, His majesty),
such glory as an only begotten son receives from his father,
full of grace (favor, loving-kindness) and truth.

JOHN 1:14 AMP

The word "tabernacle" brings to us one of the clearest revelations of the love and care of God for His people. It says to us that God has chosen to come to us in our need, to draw close in intimacy and compassion, and to cover us with His presence.

When God's people go through great hardships and heartaches we often wonder what can be said that will bring true comfort and hope. One thing we can say with strong affirmation is that God is there, in the midst of it all. This is at the heart of Jesus, our Tabernacle. Jesus didn't stay away from us, hiding from our sorrows in heaven; He came to us and tabernacled among us.

SHELTER

They are [now] before the [very] throne of God and serve Him day and night in His sanctuary (temple); and He Who is sitting upon the throne will protect and spread His tabernacle over and shelter them with His presence.

REVELATION 7:15 AMP

God reaches out to those who have come through great tribulation and spreads His tabernacle over them—the tabernacle of His presence to protect and shelter them. In the midst of our deepest sorrows, tears, and struggles God spreads the tent of His presence over us!

How close is God to us when we face our greatest trials and difficulties? The Bible tells us that God collects our tears in His bottle (Psalm 56:8). How close is God to you? No one can collect someone's tears in a bottle while standing at a distance. To be a collector of tears means that God is not even an eyelash away.

KING OF GLORY

Lift up your heads, O ye gates; and be ye lift up, ye everlasting
doors; and the King of glory shall come in.
PSALM 24:7

Think of your life as a city that is surrounded by gates. The gates
represent entrances into your heart, mind, and spirit. Think of Jesus
as a conquering King who wants to enter. He comes to conquer the
entire city—every low place, every high place, every secret place.

As the King of Glory, Jesus is strong and mighty in battle. However,
His entry into your life is not a forced entry; He enters your gates as
you throw open the doors. He manifests His strength, not by knocking
your gates down, but by conquering every enemy that has laid siege
to your life. Lift up your gates and let the King of Glory come in!

THE VINE

Yes, I am the vine; you are the branches.
Those who remain in me, and I in them, will produce much fruit.
For apart from me you can do nothing.

John 15:5 NLT

One day, when the grapes were young and ripening on the vine, a boy
watched as a bird landed on the vine and broke off a small branch. The
boy ran to the house and returned with some glue. He carefully picked
up the branch and glued it back on the vine. When the boy returned
to the vine a week later he discovered, to his disappointment,
that his glued-on branch had died and its grapes had shriveled up.
The lesson is a simple one: branches that are *on* the vine die,
while branches that are *in* the vine thrive.

Jesus is our vine. He is not just a branch, but the entire vine, our only
source of life—nourishment, growth, fullness, sweetness. In Jesus, the
sap of eternal life flows and carries with it all that we need to thrive,
to become mature, and to bear much fruit.

RABBI

Nathanael answered and saith unto him, Rabbi,
thou art the Son of God; thou art the King of Israel.
JOHN 1:49

Jesus is the King of all kings, the Lord of all lords, the Master of
all masters, the Rabbi of all rabbis, and the Teacher of all teachers.
As our Teacher, we find His teaching to be very different than most
of the teachers we have known. Jesus does not teach us so that we
can get a good education. He teaches us so that our lives will be
changed and honor His Father.

The teaching that Jesus brings points us to the Teacher, not just to facts.
Jesus' teaching brings change to the heart. Jesus, our Rabbi, does not
want us to simply gain more knowledge, but He wants us to be
transformed into His image. As your Rabbi, Jesus is saying, "Know My
words and learn of Me, learn of Me and you will become as I am."

THE BREAD OF GOD

For the bread of God is He who comes down
from heaven and gives life to the world.

JOHN 6:33 NKJV

Jesus is God's Bread. Bread is not made to be displayed, to be admired, to be studied, to be analyzed, to be compared with other breads, to be used as a centerpiece, or to be packaged. Bread is not made to educate or entertain; it is made to sustain. Bread is to be eaten.

Receive Him, eat of Him, delight in Him, partake of Him. He is fresh Bread, daily Bread. Take as much as you can, again and again. There will always be enough and more than enough.

Bread of Heaven, feed me...nourish my soul...fill my hunger...be my strength. Be in every fiber of my being, in every heartbeat, in every longing, in every hope, in every work, in every step, in every plan, in every purpose.

PHYSICIAN

And when the Pharisees saw it, they said to His disciples, "Why does your Teacher eat with tax collectors and sinners?" When Jesus heard that, He said to them, "Those who are well have no need of a physician, but those who are sick."

MATTHEW 9:11-12 NKJV

Jesus is like no other physician you will ever visit. As your Great Physician, Jesus examines you and then prescribes Himself as the way to get well. He is the best thing that could ever happen to your body, your soul, your mind, and your emotions. He can bring healing to every area of your life that needs to be made whole.

As your Physician, Jesus has faced every form of heartache and human emotion. He was a man of sorrows and knows how to lift your heavy burden. He experienced pain and knows how to touch every hurt within your heart. He knows how to turn your ashes into beauty, and your mourning into joy.

JESUS, NAME ABOVE ALL NAMES

Therefore, God elevated him to the place of highest
honor and gave him the name above all other names,
that at the name of Jesus every knee should bow,
in heaven and on earth and under the earth.

PHILIPPIANS 2:9-10 NLT

All that our hearts have ever desired, every need we face, every truth we seek, and every blessing we long for is found in Jesus Christ. There is no other person, no other relationship, no other provision, and no other source that God will use to meet our deepest needs.

All things are in Jesus Christ, and we are complete in Him. He is the Fountain that quenches our thirst, the Bread that nourishes our souls, the Light that dispels our darkness, the Physician that heals our wounds, the Shepherd that guides our steps, the Counselor that gives us wisdom, the Word that establishes us in truth, the Faithful One that gives us security, the Vine that nourishes our spirits, the Dayspring that gives us hope, the Door that gives us access to the Father, and the Mighty God that rules our hearts.

ALL IN ALL

Christ is all, and in all.
COLOSSIANS 3:11

Although it has only three letters, the word "all" has huge implications. "All" means total, complete, or whole. In a baseball game, if one team scored all the runs it means the other team scored none. If one candidate received all the votes in an election it means the other candidate received none. If a doctor tells you to take all of your antibiotics it means he doesn't want any left over.

Jesus is the "all" of God, it means that God has eliminated every other option. Jesus Christ is God's all—all God's fullness, all God's treasures of wisdom and knowledge, all God's authority, all God's power, all God's blessings. All God's promises are yours today if you are in Christ. God has no other plan, no other purpose, no other provision, and no other person for you other than Jesus Christ.

These have been written so
that you may believe that Jesus
is the Christ, the Son of God;
and that believing you may
have life in His name.

JOHN 20:31 NASB